GIRL.

poems about sexuality & gender

ALSO BY ROBIN WILLIAMS

In the Mid-Hours
Sinful Atticus
Scars of Apollo

GIRL.

Querencia Press, LLC
Chicago Illinois

QUERENCIA PRESS

LIBRARY OF CONGRESS CATALOG-IN-PUBLICATION DATA

ISBN 979-8-9860788-1-6

www.querenciapress.com

First Published in 2022

Querencia Press, LLC
Chicago IL

Printed & Bound in the United States of America

I feel like I'm lying to myself, simply because I haven't a single understanding over who I am. I don't know what I want, I don't know how I feel, and the only comfort is knowing that gender and sexuality are fluid. I can exist in this fluidity without certainty, without boundaries, without a label, no matter what anyone tells me. I can just be, and that would be enough. You can just be, and that would be enough.

Content Warnings for this collection:

homophobia
religious trauma

Your health comes first, always. Take care of yourselves.

Like a dove, my first sound is a coo, but it is no sign of
peace. My hands will know of nothing else but splinters from
closet doors, tucked neatly into the folds of my knuckles.
Think sea but the "s" is silent, it makes no sound, no whisper
in the waves crashing, nobody screams and nobody hears me.
My name is Robin, say it with me. R-o-b-i-n. Make the sound
of "r" again. And again. And again, until the word becomes
full in your mouth and settles on your tongue.

coo-ea-r sounds a little bit like
queer.
Close
but not enough.
I'm queer
but not enough.

The first time someone called me a faggot I only knew
the innocent definition,
I'm not a bundle of sticks I said.
The second time someone called me a faggot I knew it was to
hurt me, to spit in my eye,
But I stood there and laughed at them with blood in my smile
and fire in my veins

When you've spent so much time in the hell they've
created for you, it doesn't take long for your skin to melt
into scales.
It doesn't take long, or a second thought, to kill all those who
killed you.

type of girl

inspired by ashley frangipane *"fun girl"*

i'm a floral dresses in the middle of summer
type of girl
i'm a long hair, waxed brows type of girl
i'm a paint my nails purple type of girl
i'm a show a little skin type of girl
i'm a grew up dancing in the ballet type of
girl
i'm a hide behind my mother, too shy to talk
type of girl
i'm a hold your emotions in till combustion
type of girl
i'm a soft type of girl
i'm a wear five inch heels type of girl
i'm a can you spot check my butt for me
type of girl
i'm a

type of boy

inspired by ashley frangipane *"fun girl"*

i'm a messy hair, full brows, (read: unibrow)
type of boy
i'm a dirt under fingernails type of boy
i'm a fifteen pull-ups in a middle school gymnasium
type of boy
i'm a baggy sweats type of boy
i'm a torn sole sneakers and muddy laces
type of boy
i'm a grew up playing t-ball type of boy
i'm a treat your mother right type of boy
i'm a soft type of boy
i'm a cry at heart-warming movies type of boy
i'm a let's compare leg hair lengths type of boy
i'm a

"No, but what were you born as?"

as a demon with fangs in their mouth, who swallowed their
own tongue to keep from talking back because sweethearts
live forever, and despite being cursed as a sinner right out of
the womb, i pleaded with my creator to give me a chance

as a flower, yellow and bold, with my chin pointed up to
the light, a shelter for field mice, tired lost souls, and
pretty men, a restaurant for birds, heavy rich soil, and
gentle tongues

as a sharp silver blade, begging for a taste of spilt blood,
pale lips on straight faces

as "None of your fucking business."

*first published in Queerlings Mag Issue 5

I don't want to be a woman.

I don't want to be anything.

Lord, are you listening?
I have awoken with the
sun and singing birds
left the peace of my sleep to reach you

Lord, will you answer me?
I stand at the highest point in my damned town
stones packed into the soles of my shoes.
They tried to throw them.

The stones, they tried.
They took a page from your holy book,
smeared my blood upon it and said
it was justified because you told them to.

You told them that my existence was wrong, but
Lord, are you a liar?

You told me to love
told me to turn the other cheek and
that the son died for my sins.

So Lord,
Listen to me,
Answer me.

Why have you cast me out from your people, from
your kingdom,
simply for loving someone the way love was intended?

Waiting For God to Answer Me

if you were to ask me to write a poem about my identity i
would give you scribbled notes on the take home bulletins
from my church
that would all share the same message

god hates me and his people do too,
but i love who i love
and i'm not going to change

and the truth is, when i say i'm not going to change,
i mean it, i'm not,
and my message won't either

because for as long as i have lived,
i have never heard god answer a single one of my prayers

the first time i prayed it was for my great grandmother
who laid in a bed in a nursing home nine miles away, to
hold onto her last breath until my mother could take me
to see her

instead, he let her die,
and i took my anger out on my mom for not taking me
soon enough, my mom,
who just lost the same person i loved,
and i bet i made her feel like shit for it

the second time i prayed, i wouldn't even call
it a prayer, it was a curse,
the first swear words i remember uttering
i said,
"fuck god"
out of anger for something

while trying to stand on a ledge, on my
dresser that split my tongue with my tooth
when i slipped

my mom slapped me across the cheek and told me to
never say that again,
and drug me to church on a grey rainy morning with black
dress shoes, too tight

i don't remember why i uttered those words,
but they've resonated with me more than the
Gospel, and each time i sit in church listening to his
people sing hymns, i look up at the cracked ceiling
wondering,

God,
When will you answer me?

A Poem In Which I'm Back Under The Church Pews Twenty-One Years Later

In 2011 I took my last nap under the golden, wood church pews, playing hide and seek, laying belly down on velvety, green carpet while the parents talked on red couches under stained glass windows. It was the last time I saw a room full of once familiar faces, most of whom have all died or moved on from religion, much like I have retired from faith and water that was poured over my bald, baby head. But today, I return to the empty sanctuary, and I breathe in the dust my lungs have missed being filled with, and a million forgotten memories flood my mind.
I crawl on my stomach, back under the church pews, and I'm listening to the silence, when a giggle escapes my parted lips.
I think:
I want to marry my wife here, one day, under the high wooden beams, with golden hour light painting the stained glass on the floor
In front of all the people I knew and know,
in front of that Holy Man,
in spite
and in faith,

that I won't have to hide under a church pew again.

I've never dated a woman in my life, but I made one up in my head, like all hopeless romantics do when the books no longer fill the void and the peers at your school are too dull and real for your liking.

But I fell in love with one, on the kindergarten playground with mulch in my light up sketchers. I knew I loved her when I sat under the mud stained, yellow playset and watched her run off with some boy, with my brows furrowed in annoyance, and a feeling in my stomach that could only be described as jealousy.

I went home and told my parents some new boy showed up in class and took my best friend away. Granted, I may have just been lonely, a child with one close friend, but little Robin Elizabeth would remember that girl until they met again a decade later.

And little Robin Elizabeth would hold a grudge against that boy well after he moved away.

Because not only did she lose her best friend to another home, but she lost the one person she could blame her hurt upon, and she was again

A child, alone, with love and hurt in the palms of her hands, unsure of what to do with it.

I'm in love with her
but she is
the water cupped in my hands, trickling dry between the
cracks of my fingers.
Something I can only hold for a moment
and a moment

is never enough.

As a child, the fascination with fabric and thread earned me an A+ in home economics and a pride in my skill to follow a pattern. As a teen, I learned to patch the torn pieces of myself with someone else's skin, wiped the blood on my ripped skinny jeans and moved on with a pinned up smile. I continued with the needle until I was a Sally's dress of a person, a rainbow of skin, but I still didn't feel welcomed.

OPEN CALL: LOOKING FOR A GIRLFRIEND

Requirements: I'd prefer it/if you were ace too/asexual, you know/as it's part of who I am/and I don't want there to be complications if I tell you no/so you must respect that/and also/you must be patient/not all the time/but when we're out and about/I might need a moment to catch my breath/because I have social anxiety/and also/you will need to be pretty/and by pretty/I mean you must be nice/and respectful/and treat my sister right/treat my friends right/treat the waitress at our table right/there is ugliness in disrespect that isn't called for

Will Receive: poetry/not right away/and maybe just a draft that isn't all that good/but you will get something about you/and you'll get presents, too/I'm incapable of holding money/if I'm with someone I love/I want to treat them/so I buy them/something nice/like flowers maybe/or gas money/or a trinket you never asked for/and you should know that I'm impulsive/though I'm trying to work on it/it's one of my toxic traits/I'm rash/but I will love you/perhaps in a way no one ever has/I will love you forever/even if forever/is not what we want/in the end

will i find love if i remove asexual from my
dating bio, remove the first line their eyes
lay upon?
will people swipe right instead of left,
if i stay silent about the identity that has given
me the most of nothing?

i admit
i am tired of feeling the pain in my chest
when i ask them
if me being ace would be a problem,
and they say   what is that
and i have to explain
and then they ghost me without another word.

i've gone so far as to leave a definition
under the word so i can spare myself the
time,
but when i asked again
they said   i read it but i didn't understand it

as if the words *no sex* were foreign to them
like the word *love* is foreign to me

when i fall into the in between
of saying i am gay
when i am bisexual
because it is simply easier to say one syllable than it is to say
four

am i falling into a pit of internal erasure?
am i adding to the pile of bones left at the bottom of the
canyon?

i argue with myself when i lay awake at night dreaming
about a future that has a man ahead of me and i shake my
head widely till the image becomes a woman, because my
dreams need to be diverse and true,
or else when i wake up, i question

am i living a lie?

this deeply rooted turmoil that weaves out and
around with my ligaments is impossible to separate
without falling apart

am i disgraceful if my bones are black, cracked, decaying with
the rest of my certainty and dare i say,

Pride?

THEY TRIED TO ERASE ME

They said I was straight because I dated a man for three years, dated two men before that, and because I hadn't kissed a woman (disregarding the fact that I would later choose to never kiss anyone). I was simply lying to myself and everyone else. They tried to erase me.

They said I was a cheater, because anyone who was attracted to more than one person was destined to have no morals, was more likely to act with betrayal and no remorse. They tried to erase me.

They said, What's the big deal? when I was outed to the team as if my most vulnerable secret wasn't skinned from my soul and put on display, as if the looks the girls gave me didn't scare anyone else. They tried to erase me.

They said it was just a phase, just girls being girls, just the internet being unsafe, just confusion, just a feeling I would soon get over, just a demon lurking in my veins, just a life without Christ, just come pray and it will all go away. They tried to erase me. They tried to erase .

if i make my world unforgettable,
if i'm a part of everyone,
if i linger with the ghosts,
in the minuscule spaces between letters, the words
they retell in a memory they think of when on a
train ride home, when the smell of cinnamon and
sugar passes under their nose, would i be, then,
eternal
if i refuse to leave?

i don't know how to hold my own heart anymore

but i don't want to give it away

not again
not yet

I FEEL SO FUCKING LONELY/I SPEND HOURS ON
HINGE/A DATING APP MEANT TO BE
DELETED/PRESSING X ON EVERY PERSON BECAUSE
I WANT THE LOVE BUT I DON'T WANT THE
COMMITMENT/I WANT THE GIRL/BUT SHE'S A
LESBIAN/AND I A BISEXUAL/ASEXUAL/DON'T FEEL
QUEER ENOUGH/FOR ANOTHER WOMAN/TO
LOVE/BUT THE MEN/ALWAYS ASK FOR A
THREESOME/AND I'M TIRED OF SAYING/NO/I'M
TIRED OF WANTING TO SAY/YES/TO END THE
CYCLE OF
REJECTION/EVEN IF I'M JUST GOING TO GET HURT
IN THE END/I ALWAYS GET HURT IN THE END/I
DON'T CARE IF I GET HURT IN THE END

I want a messy kind of love,

Without the yelling and the back and forth,
Without the coming back to each other and third and
fourth chances.

I want a messy kind of love,

The love that leaves you slumped over the bathroom sink
picking dried paint out from under your nails.
The love that lets you hang a hobby painting up in the
kitchen nook. The love that gives and stays and takes but
never breaks and remains good in every way.

I want a messy kind of love.

1. when i fell in love, i opened my mouth up wide,
filled my stomach with every last thing love had to offer.
he crawled inside, too, and made home under my tongue. i
couldn't speak a word that wasn't his name, couldn't tell a
story that wasn't ours.
and when he left me, he took none of his things, let them
collect like dust, and what was love wisped away, lost, trapped
behind my teeth

2. the ghost in my throat is afraid you'll leave
before I even have a chance to utter a plea

Bisexual: *A black out poem*

There's a kind of cage that dating a man forges when you're
bisexual.

You're   locked in   you're straight,
locked out   you're gay.

         I
              a   m
         bisexual.

                    In this poem I call my sexuality
a prison.

I'm lying to myself.

                    I'm bisexual.

I won't let *you* imprison me.
         me.

I'm bisexual.

first published in In the Mid-Hours

Love is not loved in units of measurement. I do not love you only half the time, but endlessly. I do not find attraction in percentages. I do not find them beautiful seventy-five percent, and her only twenty-five percent of the time.

There is no talk of numbers within my sexuality.
There is no less than or greater than.
There is simply... enough.

I am queer.
I am enough.

Lightning Source UK Ltd.
Milton Keynes UK
UKHW020639150522
403024UK00005B/12